Bug Out Bag

How to Make the Ultimate Bug-Out Bag

Robert Reinoehl

PUBLISHED BY:
Robert Reinoehl
Copyright © 2013

TABLE OF CONTENTS

Chapter 1: Meet BOB – the Bug-Out Bag

What is a bug-out bag?

A bug-out bag or BOB is a bag that will help you to escape and survive any disaster. It is sometimes called a GOOD bag (*Get Out Of Dodge* bag), a 72-hour kit, a PERK (*Personal Emergency Relocation Kit*), a go bag, or even a grab bag. It is a basic bag – preferably a backpack that is designed to get you from the site of a disaster to safety. It should be prepared before a disaster so that when a catastrophe strikes, you only need to grab it.

What are the key attributes of a bug-out bag?

Bug-out bags need to be light and portable. At the same time, they must contain everything you will need to survive comfortably for three days (72-hours). These two attributes are the primary features of the BOB.

Although many emergencies will allow you to evacuate in a vehicle, there are times when evacuation routes may be blocked or overburdened. In addition, some emergencies, such as an EMP pulse, may render your vehicle useless. For this reason, the BOB needs to be portable. Backpacks are the most portable sacks available.

The BOB must also contain enough gear to allow you to survive for three days. The reason is that you need to be able to get to a safe place that is far enough away from the disaster. In a vehicle, three days should be more than enough time to get you away from danger. On foot, the average person who is reasonably healthy and in good condition should be able to hike about 45 miles in three days. This is a good enough distance to reach safety in most cases.

Finally, the BOB must be portable. It must be lightweight enough to carry from place to place without causing too much fatigue. Although it is essential to have what you need, it is equally important not to carry an excessive amount of unnecessary items.

The basics of a personal survival kit

A personal survival kit is the most basic tool to help you in any disaster. Once you put together a BOB or personal survival kit, you will know that you have your own emergency insurance. You will need to check your BOB monthly and maintain it, but it will provide you with security should a disaster occur

Here are some of the items you will want to include in your BOB:

- Roll of pennies, dimes, nickels, and quarters, $20 in dollar coins, $20 in ones, and $40 in fives
- Energy bars or other food to give 7,500 calories (3 days worth of calories)
- 3 gallons water
- First aid kit (described later)
- Iodine or chlorine water purification kits
- Radio with batteries or hand crank
- Charged cell phone

- Flashlight with batteries or crank generator
- Matches, butane lighter, (optional camp stove, FireSteel, and fuel)
- Lip balm and hard candy
- Package of sanitary items for women
- Five day supply of any prescription medicines
- Three day supply of socks and underwear
- Pocketknife with saw tooth option
- Maps with evacuation routes marked and a compass
- Whistle/ three signal flares
- Light weight rain poncho
- 2 rolls duct tape
- Mess kit, travel bottle of dish soap, and rag/bandana
- Hand sanitizer
- Can opener
- Measuring spoons and 1 cup size plastic measuring cup
- Lightweight tent, tarp, or bivy sack, mallet or hammer, (optional: a tent lock)
- Sleeping bag and bed roll (your BOB can act as a pillow or use a camp pillow)
- Toilet paper
- Travel toothbrush, dental floss or tape, and toothpaste
- Pen and small notebook
- Fishing kit
- Folding shovel and ax
- Weapons or walking sticks

There may be other things you would like to include in a basic survival kit. However, this is the minimum amount of items needed for the average person. People who are used to backpacking or minimum impact campers may require fewer items than what is listed. People with special needs or small children may require more. If you do not have special needs, but would like to take additional items, you may want to create a second "optional" bag with a shoulder strap. This bag would contain non-essential items that could be abandoned if necessary but that may be difficult for you to part with initially.

Chapter 2: Choosing an Emergency Gear Bag

Backpack styles

The best style of backpack for a BOB is an internal frame pack with a hip strap. These backpacks contain a frame for support, but they do not restrict your movement like external frame backpacks do. They may not allow you to tie extra items to the frame, but you do not want to overburden yourself with bulky items anyway. You may also want to consider one that has removable straps. Should you need to check you bag in an airport somewhere, removing and storing the straps can make the process easier.

Regular backpacks do not have the added support of a hip strap. If you need to hike over long distances, they will begin to hurt your shoulders and back. The hip-strap allows you to better balance the weight and transfers it to your hips where it is easier to support. Regular backpacks also do not contain as much space for all your gear. You may find it difficult to fit everything into your BOB that you need.

There are ultra-light packs and lightweight packs, but you need to make sure that the weight you carry is less than 30 pounds if you choose either of these options. (Three-gallons of water alone can weigh up to 25 pounds.) Lightweight and ultra-light packs do not have a hip-strap. They also may not be as well-padded as an internal or external frame pack.

Size does matter

When searching for a backpack, ideally you will find one that can carry the weight of your survival items and has enough room for all your needs. If you are uncertain how much room you will need, it is better to get a larger pack than one that is too small. Packs that have been stuffed beyond their capacity are more difficult to carry than those that are under loaded. As you consume some of the food and water and use other items, your BOB will lighten, and space will clear anyway.

You also need to make sure your pack is fitted if you are purchasing an internal frame pack. Packs are sized based on the distance between the seventh cervical vertebra and the top of your hip bone. (You can find your seventh cervical vertebra by placing your fingers on your backbone at the base of your head and following your backbone down until your feel the bump at the level of your shoulders. The bump is the seventh cervical vertebra.) Some stores will help fit the pack. Keep in mind that a large in one brand of backpack may not be the same size as a large in a different brand backpack. Always go by measurements.

Key features of a BOB pack

Not only should a BOB pack be lightweight, durable, have an internal frame, and be able to carry all of your gear, there are some other important features you need to consider. You also need to load your BOB and place it on your back to adjust the straps when you first get it. Then you should bend over to stretch the pack. As you are periodically maintaining it, check the adjustments by putting it on your back. The pack should feel as if it is a part of you, and the straps should not pinch or choke you. If you have to throw the BOB on your back and go and it is not adjusted properly, you will be sore and tired, and you may lose your balance over rough terrain.

The straps on the BOB need to be adjustable and have padding. The straps should be curved and have a sternum strap that connects them over your chest to help take the load off your shoulders. There should be padding across the back – especially in the lumbar region. There also needs to be hip-straps that have adequate padding in them.

Finally, you need to make sure the contents inside your BOB stay dry. Some fabrics are naturally waterproof, but seams will need to be sealed to keep moisture out. To keep the contents of your BOB dry on the inside, you can line your BOB with a trash bag or trash compactor bag. You should also keep things like water and wet foods double bagged to prevent leaks.

Chapter 3: Water and Hydration

Metal and plastic canteens

Frequently you will find metal or plastic containers called "canteens" in wilderness sections of the store. These have been the traditional wilderness water carriers. With our modern capabilities, they are now things of the past. Both are bulky to carry, although you can buy belts on which to hook them. They also have smaller openings which will make them difficult to refill if you need to use a natural source.

Metal canteens are heavier and more difficult to carry than plastic ones. They often have shoulder straps, but it would take twelve standard sized canteens to carry enough water for three days. In addition, they can leave odd flavors in them. The benefits of a metal canteen are that they can usually be placed directly on a fire to boil the water inside them for purification, and they retain hot liquids longer than plastic containers. Metal canteens are difficult to find today. If you want one, be sure that it has been lacquered on the inside – especially if you want to carry any beverage other than water inside it.

Plastic canteens generally do not give water an odd flavor after they have been washed. They are also lighter to carry than metal ones. They cannot be placed directly into a fire, but you can still use water purification tablets or water filters. You only should store water in a plastic canteen. Plastic retains smells and flavors and can transfer the smells to your water.

Collapsible water containers and water bladders

Collapsible water containers seem as if they would be ideal for packing. Some come in five-gallon varieties, but other sizes are available. They will fold up when they are not in use. However, the five-gallon types are not designed easily to carry water from place to place. If you know you will have a water supply on your evacuation route, you could take one of these folded in your BOB. Then you could use them to collect and purify water with water purification tablets. These may also be useful if you are taking a vehicle when you evacuate. The smaller collapsible water bottles are not very durable. If you are in a disaster situation, you do not want your water supply to fail. It could cause you to be without a vital resource, and it could get your entire equipment wet in the process.

Water bladders or soft bottles are a much better option for a BOB. A water bladder is a plastic bag that comes as part of a hydration system with a flexible tube straw. These can carry the same amount or more water than a traditional canteen. They also come with convenient carriers or can be fitted into mesh pockets on some backpacks. Water bladders and hydration systems will leak if you do not secure the lid on the bottle. Soft water bottles are generally stored upright, so they are less likely to cause problems.

Another collapsible option is a water bag. These are not good for carrying water on the back. However, if you find a water source and want to make camp, they are an easy way to carry water to your camp from the water source.

Nalgene-style water bottles

Nalgene is the latest method of water carrying devices. These containers are usually clear so you can make sure they are clean on the inside. They also come with wider mouths to make it easier to refill them from a natural source. They are light to carry, but you may have to use several of them to get the required amount of water.

These are similar to canteens because they can be difficult to carry. However, they come in circular and rectangular shapes, which can help with packing. Be sure to get bottles with a loop attaching the cap to the bottle to prevent accidental loss of your cap.

Cleaning and storing water and water containers

Water containers should be washed before their first use in warm soapy water. It is also a good idea to sanitize them as well. You can use bleach water to do this effectively.

You can store water safely for long periods of time in five-gallon FDA-approved DOT #34 containers. Water should be stored in the dark. When storing water, opaque containers are better than clear ones.

If you want to store your water in BOB pack containers, you will need to replace it every three to six months. Storing bottled water is safer than storing tap water. You can also use a commercially available water preserver to increase the storage time of your water.

Water purification on the go

Water is one of the most important resources. People who are traveling by foot can need a minimum of a half-gallon of water per day and can consume up to a gallon of water each day. However, water is extremely heavy to carry.

When you are planning an evacuation root on foot, it is always a good idea to plan one that has many sources of water along it. Fresh, fast flowing water is the best. However, you can filter water that is cloudy. Make sure you use a method of purification before drinking water from natural sources. Disasters tend to lower water quality from all sources, including your home tap water.

Portable water filters and pumps

Unless you are surviving a disaster-involving radioactivity, portable water filters and pumps are often not worth the effort. Hand pumps require much effort for little water return, and gravity fed filtration systems take a long time. Also, water filters are heavy, and retain some of the water, so they can leak on your other gear after their first use. You need to make sure your filter has pore sizes of less than one micron if you want to filter out disease causing agents.

If you only need a filter to clarify cloudy water, coffee filters placed in a funnel are a quick, lightweight, and simple method of removing dirt. You can use one to three filters. The more filters you use, the slower the water will drain, but the water will be cleaner. After filtering cloudy water, you can boil it for ten minutes to kill any disease causing agents.

If you are interested in using pump or gravity water filters, you may want to place them in your "optional" bag and keep water purification tablets in your main pack.

Water purification tablets

Chlorine, iodine, and chlorine dioxide are the three top methods of tablet purification. They all come in an easy to carry tablet form. Water purification tablets are convenient and come with directions for use. Some purification systems have two steps and some come with a citrus flavor (ascorbic acid), which makes drinking the purified water more palatable.

Iodine should not be used by people with allergies to iodine or people who have problems with their thyroid. It also should not be used for more than two weeks. Chlorine dioxide is the most popular method of water purification. It is quick and effective. Some people believe it also leaves the best tasting water.

When using water purification tablets, the clarity and temperature of the water affect the time it will take to use the tablets. Be sure to follow directions carefully. Plan ahead so you do not have to thirstily sit for hours waiting for water to purify.

Purifying water after an emergency involving radiation

Radioactive emergencies spew radioactive particles into the air and water. While radioactive particles never completely mix with the water, they become suspended in it. Traditional methods of water purification will not remove these particles.

There are three methods for cleaning radioactive particles from water. The first is to use a reverse osmosis filter. These are the same filters used for desalinating seawater and other brackish water. The drawbacks are that they can be heavy and somewhat expensive. You will need to use a separate standard water filter first to clean the water of large impurities and preserve your reverse osmosis membrane if you choose this method.

The second method is to use distillation. Building a solar powered one still while traveling across country is not practical. However, you can purchase or make your own fire distiller. Keep in mind that these distillers can be heavy and bulky to carry. Also, they can be very expensive.

If you use either reverse osmosis or distillation, note that these processes remove any naturally occurring electrolytes from the water. Be sure to replace them with powdered electrolyte drink mixes to prevent your body from becoming unbalanced.

The third option is complicated, but may be the cheapest method for purifying water with radioactive particles in it while traveling. You need activated charcoal (or you can make your own from a sod smothered fire), a rope, some coffee filters, two water bottles with rigid sides (i.e., canteens), a funnel, and fine clay. Place two cups of activated charcoal into your canteen and add the water. Invert the canteen twenty times to mix it well every half hour for two to three hours. Place a coffee filter inside the funnel and carefully pour the water through it to filter it. Collect the filtered water in another canteen. Add two cups of charcoal to the filtered water. This time allows the water to sit in the closed canteen for 24 hours. Filter through another coffee filter again. Add ¼ cup dry, powdered, fine clay per two quarts of water, invert it twenty times, and allow it to sit for an hour. Attach the rope securely to the top of the canteen and spin the canteen rapidly over your head rapidly for about a minute. Filter carefully through another coffee filter, being careful not to disturb the sediment at the bottom of the canteen. Boil the water for ten minutes to remove any disease causing agents before drinking it.

Chapter 4: Food and Food Preparation

Food supplies to go

The key to food for your BOB is that it should be lightweight and compact. You should not take canned foods and foods in boxes should be removed from the box and placed in a plastic zipper bag.

Here are some examples of survival foods suitable for your BOB:

- Candy Bars, Carbohydrate/ Energy Bars, Granola Bars,
- MREs
- Dehydrated foods
- Prepackaged store foods

Survival diet needs

The most important thing for your survival food to do is to give you enough energy to get from the site of the disaster to a place of safety. However, you also do not want to pack much weight. You may want to eat some hot food as you leave the disaster area – especially if you are going to be traveling when it is cold. If you choose hot food, you will need a source to heat it, such as a camp stove or fire, and you will also need containers, such as a mess kit, in which to heat it. If you are going to be traveling through hot areas, you may decide that hot food is not worth the extra weight.

The minimum amount of calories an average 5' 8" person needs per day is 2,500. However, you may want to insure you have between 3,000 and 5,000 calories per day. The minimum calories will prevent you from starving, but if you have to hike your way out you will probably lose weight eating only the minimum calories required per day. The maximum amount of calories will cause your BOB to weigh more, but you will not be hungry.

It is best to pack so that you either do not have to stop for lunch or so that you only stop long enough to sit down and eat. It is also a good idea to pack items for dinner that are easy to prepare. They make camp ovens, and there are many different cookbooks with gourmet recipes for the road, but you are trying to escape a disaster situation and need to put as much distance between you and the site of the emergency as quickly as you can.

Although you should pack food for speed, you also need to pack for palatability. Always try the foods you are packing before you add them to your BOB. If you pack foods that need preparation, you should prepare them as if you were in a survival situation. This will help you judge if they are worth the added effort or not.

Special dietary needs

There are many camp foods available that meet the needs of people with special dietary considerations. It is also easy to make your own prepackaged meals. If you are vegetarian or vegan, there are plenty of meat free trail foods. If you are diabetic, there are foods with lower carbs.

You can also make your own trail mixes from nuts,

chocolate, and dried fruits based on your dietary considerations. Keep in mind, if you are on a low sodium diet that you should take some salt along to balance the amount of sodium lost when you sweat.

For babies, you can take powdered cereal and powdered formula and store single-serving sizes in plastic baggies.

Nutrition in a Bar

There are several energy bars, candy bars, and granola bars that provide nutrition and energy for traveling. Bars tend to be fairly balanced, high in calories, and low in weight. They also take up little room in your pack. A person in a survival situation with a BOB containing enough bars to meet their calorie needs will do fine.

The downside of eating only bars is that your body tends to get tired of the flavor and texture quickly. Although bars come in a variety of flavors, they all begin to taste the same after extended use.

When selecting the type of bar to pack, you should consider several factors. Candy bars should be the kind made from chocolate. Candy bars that do not contain chocolate are pure sugar. You will burn through this energy quickly and soon feel starving. When you eat candy bars that do not contain chocolate, you will end up eating more calories than what you need without feeling as satisfied. In addition, try to find a candy bar that contains nuts. Nuts are an excellent source of protein. There are some candy bars that are mostly nuts and do not have chocolate in them; these candy bars are okay to pack as well. A few candy bars contain fruit, such as raisins; these are also a good choice.

Granola bars have been a survival mainstay for years.

They come in both chewy and crunchy textures. You can choose whichever texture you prefer. Try to stay away from granola bars that are dipped in chocolate. Many times these have high sugar content and a low caloric value. Like candy bars, granola bars with nuts and fruit are better than those that are plain.

Energy bars are designed for hiking. Energy bars have different textures and different tastes. Some are better than others. These bars will provide you with all your calorie needs, but you need to try them before packing them in your sack. Try to find two or three different kinds of energy bars that you like. You can usually find them in the health food, diet, or vitamin section of your local store.

Mess-kits
Carrying pots, pans, silverware, plates, bowls, and cups in a BOB can take up space and weight you down. The best option to resolve all your eating needs is to purchase a mess kit. Mess kits may or may not contain silverware; you can purchase special travel silverware or just pack some plastic forks and spoons. A mess kit general comes with a pan, a plate, and a cup all made out of lightweight aluminum. Because they are made to serve one person, you can just rinse them out and scour them with a dishcloth. You can boil water in them to sterilize them. You should take it apart, wash it, and put it back together before packing it.

MREs and dehydrated foods

MREs, or meals ready to eat, were developed by the military to feed soldiers in the field. Occasionally the government will also use them to help at disaster sites. They are easy to pack and easy to prepare, but they are not marketed to the general public. Online, you can find a MRE black-market. The trouble with purchasing them online is that the MREs sold are sometimes old packages that have been stored improperly. Other times you are not buying an MRE with government standards, but an off-brand. When you are trying to escape a disaster situation in a hurry, you do not want to end up with tainted food. It is not recommended you use MREs for this purpose.

A better option than MREs is the numerous dehydrated meals offered by camping supply stores as specialty backpacking food. These are packages in high calorie packages that only require you to add water. They come in varieties that range from lasagna to enchiladas. They are light to carry and relatively easy to make. The down side is that they can be expensive. If you are a picky eater, however, this may be your best option. You can try the foods and see what you like before stocking your pack.

In addition to dehydrated backpacking food, you can also find a variety of "just add water" food in the supermarket. You can purchase inexpensive soup, bullion, rice, and noodle meals that are similar to the dehydrated backpacking meals. You should also buy dehydrated electrolyte drink mixes, coffee, hot chocolate, and dehydrated milk (if you feel you need milk), or if any of your dehydrated foods require you to "add milk." When packing prepackaged items that have not been designed to travel in a pack, you will need to transfer any items that come in boxes, tins, or glass containers in single serving, labeled, baggies. Tuna fish sold in pouches is also a good option for meat. Always take a plastic bag of salt to help keep your electrolytes in balance. Pepper and garlic are other good seasonings for the trail.

If you would prefer to make your own food from scratch, there are more options available. When looking for dried foods you can purchase dried fruits and vegetables, but you can also purchase baking mixes, such as those for pancakes, that just require you to add water. Be sure to put boxed items pre-measured into individual serving sized baggies. Other suitable dried foods are staples such as oatmeal, sugar, instant potatoes, and powdered eggs. You can make your own granola mix and trail mix as well.

Whatever food you decide to take, be sure to rotate it in and out of your BOB every three or four months, so it stays fresh. In addition, when you are escaping a disaster, never try to save your leftover food. Try to eat everything you have made, and do not save prepared food until the next meal.

Cooking pots

A cooking pot over an open fire may seem like the emergency ideal. However, unless you are going to be exiting the disaster area with several other people, carrying a cooking pot can be more weight than it is worth. A single traveler would never need to make more than one serving at a time.

A cooking pot will increase the weight in one person's pack. You must choose the person who is going to carry the cooking pot, and then you must never loose track of that person. This can cause problems when disasters separate families and friend groups. If you do decide to take a cooking pot, be sure to use one that is made from aluminum or a combination of aluminum and steel.

Campfire Cooking

If you are planning on making a campfire, you will have the benefit of a lighter pack. Campfires do not require you to carry any fuel with you. However, you will have to gather fuel and tinder. Starting a campfire in the rain is also a challenge.

You can cook on a campfire without any special equipment. All you need to do is set the pan on the side of the fire so it can still get air. If you rather would have a more advanced set up, you can learn how to make tripods and other supports online. Practice making these before you get in an emergency situation. You should be able to make working equipment from memory if you are planning on using it during an emergency.

Campfire cooking is also an acquired skill. While making soups is relatively easy, other foods can be trickier. The campfire has one heat setting – hot. You can adjust the temperature of your heat by moving your pot closer or further from the fire. You can also heat rocks and rake them away from the fire. Then you can set your pot on top of them to cook. If you are a novice at campfire cooking, it is recommended that you choose soups or meals that simply require boiling water to prepare them.

Whenever you are finished with a campfire and ready to move to your next location, dump water on it until it stops sizzling. The water does not have to be drinking water. Be careful not to burn yourself during this process. The fire will give off hot ash, smoke, and steam and may require several gallons of water to extinguish it.

Portable Stoves

Portable stoves add weight to your BOB because you have to carry fuel with them. However, portable stoves are easy to light even in the worst storm, and they will stay lit as long as you use a wind guard when you are cooking with them.

Portable stoves come in parts or fold to fit easily in your BOB. However, they are small and accommodate only small pots and pans. Make sure your mess kit and any pot you may take will fit on top of your stove.

Although portable stoves are easy to carry from one place to the next, never use one inside a sealed tent. Fire eats oxygen. You do not want to be in a closed space competing for air with a fire. The fire will always win.

Fueling the fire

Each type of stove uses a different type of fuel. Some stoves will use several fuels, but you need to make sure the fuel you use will work in your stove. For a BOB, the best type of stove/fuel is one that uses dry fuel. Dry fuel stoves burn pellets. These are lighter than other fuels and less dangerous. You also will not need to worry about your fuel leaking all over your food, clothes, and other survival items. You can even make your own (with a windscreen).

If you want to use the easy burn pellets without carrying a metal stove in your BOB, you can simply dig a small hole in the ground where you will stick the pellet. Place two to four rocks around the outside of the hole where you can balance your pan over the fire. Place a pellet in the hole, and place the pan on top of the rocks.

You may still need a wind screen if the wind is strong, but you also may be able to invent a natural one.

Some cook stoves are designed to burn fuel you find as well as dry fuel. These are the best option for a BOB bag. They will allow you to use sticks and tinder from the area when conditions are good and fuel is available, but they will also allow you to burn dry fuel when it is rainy and fuel is scarce. If you choose to pack this kind of stove, you need to be especially careful that you douse everything in water when you are finished cooking. After you are certain the unit is no longer hot, you may dump the contents of the stove, dry it, and repack it.

Protecting your food supply

If you have to escape from a disaster on foot, you need to keep in mind that the animals in the area are looking for food. Your BOB will appeal to them and be an easy target in the night. It is always best to hang you BOB from a tree at night. It should be 12 feet off the ground and 10 feet away from any tree trunk to keep it safe.

There are specially made bear sacks that also do a good job of keeping your supplies safe if their directions are followed properly. These will also need to be hung, but do not need to be so high.

It is also a good idea never to take food into or near your shelter. Hungry animals will hunt by smell and may not realize the food is no longer there. Never save food from one meal to the next. This not only attracts unwanted pests but also can make you sick without proper storage facilities.

Fishing kits

Fishing can be a good way to supplement your food supply when you are running low. However, keep in mind that fishing takes time and skill. You need to balance your food needs with the schedule you have set for yourself. You also need to practice your skill fishing and know what the fish along your evacuation route like to eat.

There are many basic, lightweight, fishing kits on the market. It is easy to buy one of these and then adjust them as you become a more experienced angler. You can catch fish with only some fishing line, a hook, a sinker, some bait (like a worm or grub), and a stick. You only should plan on using a stick you have modified as a pole (make sure it is strong or freshly cut). For this reason, you may want to practice your fishing skills this way if you would like to fall back on fishing as a way of supplementing your survival food.

What to eat if you run out of food
Scavenging for food is a time consuming process. It is best to take enough food to last three days in your BOB. However, things can happen on the trail that may cause you to go through more food than what you expected, or it may take longer to get to your destination. If you run out of food for a few days, you will not die. However, your body may not want to keep walking. You must balance mind over matter and press forward to your destination first and foremost.

If you find berries and nuts along the trail, do not eat them unless you have been trained by a professional to identify edible natural foods. Many plants – wild carrot and hemlock, for example – that are edible look similar to plants that are deadly. If you have taken a course and learned about edible plants, you should only eat those plants you know and have positively identified in the past.

Mushrooms are another dangerous wilderness food. It is best to leave all mushrooms alone. If you have been trained to identify and find mushrooms, keep in mind that location can determine whether the mushroom is edible. A mushroom that is edible when grown in one soil can make you sick when grown in another. Be very careful when using these for food supplements even if you know what you are doing.

The best way to supplement your diet while escaping a disaster is to fish. Fishing takes time, but it allows you to sit in one spot and conserve your energy. Fish also is easy to cook over a fire. If you do not like fish or if you are allergic to it, you can learn how to make snares for small animals online or in workshops. Making a snare will cause you to remain in one place for a long time, though, so balance your hunger with that time.

Chapter 5: Clothing

Clothing guidelines

Clothing is not something that you need to pack in your BOB. However, the clothing you wear when you are planning on leaving is important. Disasters can occur at any time, so it is a good idea to keep a spare BOB outfit ready by your BOB. This way you have appropriate clothing to change into for a three-day journey without having to take time to find it.

When choosing an outfit, it is best to layer your clothing. You should have an inner layer that wicks moisture away from your body. Cotton is not a good choice for the layer of clothing that touches your skin. Silk, wool, and synthetics are the best options. The next layer is your mid-layer. This layer should be made from wool or synthetics. The final layer is your protective layer. This consists of clothing that will protect you from rain, snow, sleet, and wind. The materials you choose for this layer need to be both waterproof and breathable.

The clothing you choose should be practical and should take into account weather, climate, and the terrain of your evacuation route. Although the outfit that you choose to wear can probably be set aside, outerwear like coats may need to be used in your daily life. Keep these items together near the door.

Weather appropriate clothing

Weather is changeable. Never rely on a weather report to determine what you will wear. The weatherman could say that it is going to be sunny for the next week, and it may rain. Wearing appropriate clothing means that you prepare for weather that would be typical of your environment. If you live in a desert, you will not need to wear a snowsuit. You also will not need raingear – even though it occasionally rains in the desert.

People who live in climates that change from hot to cold depending on the season will need to change their BOB outfit to match the season.

If you have a special BOB outfit, keep in mind that it should take less than five minutes to change into it. In some cases, you may not be able to change clothes at all. To be prepared, you can keep the clothing in you "optional" bag.

Footwear

One of the most important things you need if planning on walking for any amount of time is good footwear. Even if you have a vehicle to take you from one place to the next, you can never tell when roads will be blocked or flooded after an emergency. If you only have time to change one article of clothing, make sure you are wearing sensible walking shoes.

Hiking boots are the best footwear if you are in a survival situation. Hiking boots cover your feet and ankles, providing extra support. If you are going to invest in a hiking boot, know that they come in lightweight, mid-weight, and heavyweight (leather) styles. Lightweight and mid-weight should be suitable for a three-day escape. The heavier the weight of boot, the longer they will take to break in, the more durable they will be, and the warmer they will be.

While hiking boots are the best option, the right pair of shoes can be substituted in emergencies. The next best option is a pair of running or jogging shoes or hiking shoes or sandals. These will not give you the ankle support or protection of hiking boots; however, they will provide your foot the support it needs over long distances.

Tennis shoes, basketball shoes, and fashion footwear are not designed to support your foot over long distances. These should be avoided if possible.

To break in your shoes, you need to walk about fifty miles in them. It is best to walk across all sorts of terrain, but even wearing them to work for a week or two will help. If you can, put your BOB on your back and try to get in a couple of walks in the park on footpaths or grass instead of the sidewalks. Never wear a new shoe in a survival situation.

It is also a good idea to waterproof you shoes or hiking boots. Seams are never waterproofed and should be sealed as soon as you purchase your footwear. Some shoes and boots claim to be waterproof; however, it is always a good idea to waterproof them yourself as well. There are a variety of waterproofing sprays, water-based applications, and waxes for shoes and boots. Follow the directions on the container and reapply at least once a year.

Shirts

Shirts always should have the ability to be unzipped, unsnapped, or unbuttoned at least down to chest level.

They should also have high collars. These features will allow you to better control your internal temperature while you are on the move.

You should also choose a shirt with long sleeves. Long sleeves not only provide you with protection from the sun, but they also provide you with protection from scrapes and cuts. If it is warm, you should be able to roll up the sleeves.

Pockets are another positive feature of shirts. If you have pockets, you can put snacks, maps, and other essential items in reach without digging through your BOB for them.

Pants
Whether to wear pants or shorts is a decision that requires more than knowledge of the weather. Pants can provide protection to your legs if the terrain is rough or from bushes. They can also provide protection from sunburn. However, shorts allow you to move more freely than pants, and they can be worn comfortably even in colder, dry weather. Because weather changes rapidly, it might be best to wear a pair of pants over a pair of shorts or wear one and pack the other. You can also choose convertible pants with legs that unzip to form shorts. If you get convertible pants, be sure to try them on first for comfort (the zippers can rub your legs) and fit.

Whether you choose pants or shorts, pockets are a good option for either. Also, elastic waistbands are less confining than belts. Nylon pants with moisture wicking abilities are a good choice of fabric.

The importance of spare socks and underwear

Your feet and crotch collect dampness and bacteria. In addition, if you step in puddles or have to walk through water as you evacuate, your feet can become soaked. Spare socks and underwear can prevent you from developing infections and long-term and potentially life-threatening problems.

Although you will not need to bring extra outer clothes, you should plan on changing your socks and underwear every day. Bringing three pairs of each will insure that you always have a dry pair. You can wash and dry dirty pairs at night to keep a fresh supply. If they are not dry in the morning, you can attach them to the outside of your BOB as long as you are not traveling through brush and it is not raining.

Jackets and outerwear
Even if you live in the desert, temperatures in the evening can drop. You should carry or wear outerwear that is designed to handle the worst conditions for the season and environment.

The main purpose of outerwear is to keep the rain, snow, and wind away from your insulating clothing and body. There are several products on the market that do this. You should look for outerwear that is not only weatherproof but also breathable. Non-breathable outerwear may prevent the elements from getting in to you, but it will not allow your sweat, condensation, and other body moisture to get out. Even on dry days, you will be wet and uncomfortable if you are traveling in non-breathable outerwear.

Aside from protecting you from the elements, outerwear can also provide warmth depending on what type of lining it has. It can also provide some warmth.

Down fill and fleece are the warmest materials available.

Keep in mind that outerwear you plan on using in case of emergency does not only have to be worn for emergencies. Purchase high-quality outerwear and then use it every day. Ensure that your outerwear is in good condition at all times and replace it as needed. Spending extra money on quality outerwear can mean the difference between surviving a disaster and dying of exposure.

Hats, bandanas, and umbrellas

Hats are important for many reasons: they keep the rain off, they keep the sun off, and they keep you warmer. It is a good idea to carry one hat that will keep your head warm at night when you are sleeping, as well as a hat to keep the sun and rain off during the day.

Stocking caps made from fleece, wool, or synthetic materials are the best. The cap you choose should cover your ears or at least have the option of doing this. Unless you will be trekking through cold weather, you will not need a windproof hat. The hat should be breathable, and it should fit. Do not settle for "one-size fits all" without trying it on first.

Rain and sun hats need to have a brim. You do not have to go to the trouble of purchasing and wearing a sombrero to keep out the sun, a sun hat can be as simple as a baseball cap with a bandana draped over your head and neck under it. If you purchase a hat for the sun, be sure that it will also work in the rain or make sure your outerwear comes with a hood.

Umbrellas can be useful for keeping both the sun and rain off you. Although they may seem to be awkward to carry, they will do a better job than hats. The downside of umbrellas is that they do not stand up well in windy conditions. You may want to keep one in your "optional" bag.

Every BOB should have a bandana or two in it. Bandanas have unlimited use. You can wear them on your head to keep away deerflies, and they can protect your neck from the sun. You can use them to clean dishes, or you can use them to soak up the dew from the ground in the morning and get a drink of water. You can use them to help splint a broken bone, bandage a cut, or brace a sprained ankle. You can use a bandana as a potholder, a handkerchief, a towel, or a washcloth. Be sure you do not leave this valuable article of clothing at home.

Protecting your eyes
Your eyes are a valuable asset in any emergency. Protecting them is important. When your eyes are exposed to direct sunlight, it can cause cataracts, eye cancer, photokeratitis (sunburned cornea), and snow blindness. You should include a pair of sunglasses as a part of your BOB gear.

Sunglasses should be used at all time when you are outdoors in the bright sun – summer and winter. They should be certified to protect your eyes from 100% UVA and UVB rays at 400nm (sometimes labeled UV400). Sunglasses with green, gray, and brown lens are the best because they allow you to see better and with less distortion than lenses of other colors. Polarized lenses are also beneficial.

Protecting your hands
Like the rest of your body, your hands also need layers.

An inner liner-style glove is important for keeping your hands warm. Fleece and silk are good fabrics for glove inner layers. The outer glove layer should be protective and durable. Leather is a good choice of material for outer gloves. The outer-layer can be worn alone if you need to do jobs that would scratch your hands, such as pushing through bushes or collecting firewood.

Chapter 6: Shelter and Protection

Shelter options

You have three basic shelter types you can pack in your BOB: bivy sacks, tarps, and tents. The type of shelter you choose will depend on how you answer several questions.

- What type of shelter do you feel most comfortable using?

- How skilled are you at setting up your shelter?

- Do you have special family needs?

If you feel uncomfortable sleeping in the open, you will need a tent. If, on the other hand, you do not like to be closed in at all, you might prefer a tarp. If you do not want to take time to set something up, you should choose the bivy sack.

Temporary shelters made from tarps or tents need to be set up before you can use them. You always should practice setting up your shelter in your backyard or a park before a disaster happens. Do not just practice in daylight. You should also practice at night with flashlights.

For the tarps and tents, you will need these items:

- Tent (lightweight and fitting the season) or tarp.
- Nylon cord (if using a tarp)
- Locks that will fit your tent (if you are using a tent)
- Mallet or hammer
- Ax (if you are using a tarp)

If you have small children, you should choose a tent. Tents will help keep your children from wandering off. They also provide more protection and can make your children feel safer when their world is unstable. If you have pets, you may want to choose a tent to keep them from wandering off, but you can also tether them at night. If you have elderly people in your family, you will need to choose something to make them feel more comfortable. This may mean that you need to pack large self inflating mattresses and a foldable camp chair to keep them off the ground.

If something happens to your shelter, look around for shelters as you are hiking away from the disaster. You should begin looking for uninhabited buildings, uninhabited caves, bush you can crawl under, or anything that will give you some protection. Abandoned vehicles also make good shelters if you see any. However, never use a building that has been structurally damaged from a disaster as a shelter. You always should inspect a building to see if has damaged and may collapse. You do not want to be under it when it does.

Bivy sacks

A bivy sack (bivouac bag) is simply a waterproof bag that you slip over your sleeping bag. It is the crudest of shelters and only offers protection from the elements. Bivy sacks require no set up, and some of them double as raincoats. Some have mosquito netting, so you do not have to close them all the way to keep the bugs out.

If you choose a bivy sack for your BOB, make sure that it is made entirely from breathable material (some have breathable material only on the top). You also need to ensure it is a perfect fit for your sleeping bag. If it is too small, you will be cramped. If it is too large, you will be cold.

While bivy sacks are efficient and lightweight, many people will find them too open. People who are used to the shelter of a home may find it hard to transition to sleeping under the stars. This also would not be the best choice for people with young children, who may wander off without some sort of walled structure around them.

Tarps

Tarps are lightweight, cost relatively little, and allow you to cook while under your shelter if you tilt one corner upward. You will be able to see everything that is going on around you, which can be beneficial in an emergency. The problem with tarps is that they are difficult to set up and even experienced people have trouble setting one up in a wind. They also let in the wind and bugs.

If you choose to use a tarp for your shelter, you will need to pack mosquito netting, nylon rope, tent stakes, and an ax as well. You will also need to practice turning the tarp into a shelter in several formations so that you can adapt your shelter to fit your needs, should the time arise.

If you choose a tarp for your shelter, it can be used for

other purposes as well. You can cover your pack and yourself with it in a rainstorm to keep yourself dry. You can place it on the ground to eat.

Tents

Tents give you a portable home. They have ceilings and walls to keep out the elements and provide a sense of protection. They can help you reign in tired children. However, they also have to be assembled and weigh more than other options.

Tents come in all shapes and sizes. You should have the store set up your tent before you decide which one would be right for you. Tents should be fitted to your needs without being too large. You want to ensure everyone will be able to sleep inside the tent or that each person has an individual one-person tent. Again, if you have individual tents and you become separated from the rest of your group, you will still have shelter. However, a small child will not be able to set up an individual tent and will not want to sleep alone in it.

Tents are also designed for different seasons. Purchasing a three-season tent will get you through most disasters. Winter tents are designed for the special needs of camping in winter.

Every year, you should seal the seams on your tent. You should also count the tent stakes and make sure they are all there. If you take extra of anything, you should carry 2 – 3 extra tent stakes. They are easy to lose. Tent stakes come for hard ground, soft ground, and snow/sand. When you practice setting up your tent, you will discover if you have the right kind of stakes for your area.

Sleeping bags, bed rolls, and sleeping pads

Sleeping pads are important BOB items. Even in the warmth of summer, laying on the ground can be uncomfortable and can pull heat from your body quickly. Without a sleeping pad, you can wake up cold and stiff – not a good way to begin a day of escaping disaster. Sleeping pads come as foam rolls and air mattress pads. Unless you are elderly or have elderly people traveling with you, you will not need a thick mattress-sized air pad. Instead, find a thin self-inflatable one.

Bedrolls work well if you live in a warmer area with little temperature variation. To make a bed roll, you simply need to lay out a full-sized blanket and place a sheet on top. Then fold the blanket in half over the sheet lengthwise. Fold in half once more the same way and then, beginning at one end, roll the blanket/sheet up. Use small cords to tie your roll.

A sleeping bag is like a tent in that it comes designed for the season. If you have especially cold nights, you should choose a mummy sack sleeping bag. If you do not, choose a tapered sleeping bag without a hood. When you are selecting a sleeping bag, you also need to consider whether you are hot or cold when you sleep. If you normally sleep with four or five blankets on you, you should choose a mummy bag. If you normally sleep with only a sheet, choose a tapered bag.

You should also consider packing your bag with a silk liner inside it or a sheet. Sheet and liners keep you warmer by creating layers. You can also sleep with layers of clothing on or in your bag for added warmth.

Space blankets and pillows

"Space" blankets or "emergency" blankets in their purest form are plastic film sprayed with metallic paint. They are not durable, and are so difficult to refold you may find yourself wishing it was a map. They are sometimes called "emergency" blankets, but this does not mean you should use them in emergencies. Instead, it means if it is an emergency and you have absolutely nothing else to use, these will be better than nothing. If you have packed your BOB bag with the other recommended survival items, you will not need a space blanket.

Space blankets are supposed to reflect heat and wetness back to your body to keep you "warmer." They do not provide you with any insulation from your surroundings. If the ground is cold and you place the space blanket on it, the space blanket will turn instantly cold. They will also keep you wetter.

If you feel you absolutely must carry a space blanket, you can use it on top of your sleeping bag. Most space blankets are one time use, so pick the coldest night to open it up. If you want something a little better quality that is still frequently labeled a "space" blanket of some sort, you should look for a fleece style blanket with metallic coating on one side. These will last longer and keep you warmer in the end. They can also double as tarps or ground cloths.

Pillows are unnecessary in a survival situation because you can use your BOB as a pillow, or some of your clothing. However, if you want to be more comfortable when you are going through a rather uncomfortable situation all around, they make several camping pillows that are small and light weight.

Chapter 7: Making a Fire

How do I start a camp fire?

Making a campfire looks easier to do than what it is. It is important to practice making, lighting, and maintaining a fire before a situation arises where you will need to do so. Practicing your skills in dry weather, wet weather, and at night is also important, since you never know when you will need them.

The first thing you will need to do in order to start a campfire is to build a fire ring. The job of a fire ring is to prevent the spread of fire. Use a shovel or hammer to clear away grass and flammable material from the ground in a 3-foot circle. Use rocks or broken bricks to make a ring at the edge of the circle.

You should use one of the three basic campfire formations to begin your fire: the log cabin, the A-frame, and the bonfire.

In order to build the A-frame, an easy method of creating a fire, you need to make a pile of tinder the size of a baseball. On the edges of this pile build an "A," or triangle, out of twigs thinner than a pencil. As soon as you have the walls of twigs about two-inches tall, begin using thumb-sized twigs. At four-inches tall, add thicker sticks, about one-inch in diameter. When each of the three sides has two one-inch sticks, carefully poke a match through a gap the walls near the base to light the tinder. As the fire builds and gains strength, the one-inch sticks will catch on fire. Once this happens, you should add four-inch logs in the same A-shaped pattern. As the four-inch logs catch, you can add one smaller split log. At this time, you do not have to follow the pattern. Do not throw a log directly on top of the fire or it will smother it. Instead, you can position the log, so it is only covering one side.

For the bonfire method, which is another easy method, you arrange the tinder in the center, and then place thin long twigs in a teepee formation around it, pointing to the sky. Add slightly larger, thumb-sized twigs, and then light the tinder inside the formation. Once the larger twigs catch fire, add four-inch logs, being careful not to suffocate or crush the fire. Continue adding larger pieces of wood.

Fire kit
You fire kit should contain:

- Waterproof matches in a waterproof container,

- A camp stove

- Appropriate stove fuel (if necessary),

- A butane lighter,

- A FireSteel,

- Some kind of fire-starter – like fire paste or cotton balls soaked in petroleum jelly.

It is important to keep your fire kit dry, so you may want to pack it in its own zippered plastic baggie.

Matches should be carried in a waterproof container designed to carry them and then placed inside the baggie.

Getting a spark

To light any fire, you need a spark. The regular method of starting a fire is to use matches, but sometimes it is better to use a butane lighter. You should have at least one back-up method of starting any fire. If you choose to use waterproof matches, carry the lighter as a back up.

Butane lighters will throw sparks that you can use to start a fire even after they have run out of fuel. However, lighters can also be tricky for some people to use. Remember you should practice building and lighting a fire with the methods you will use in a disaster situation. Try to light a fire from the sparks butane lighters throw without pressing the button to release the fuel, as well.

There are other ways to start fires without matches, such as flint and steel kits or by rubbing two pieces of wood together, but these can be tricky and require much more practice. The only other recommended method of starting fires during emergencies is a FireSteel. The fire steel comes with a small rod and a striker. When you hit the two together they throw out hot sparks (be careful. They work in any weather, so you can start a fire even if it is pouring down rain. As with other methods of starting fires, always carry a back up plan and always practice before the disaster.

Tinder

You can use paper, dry pine needles, and small twigs (no bigger than the width of three pine needles).

Pinecones can also be used, but initially they can cause problems when you try to light them.

Dry wood and tinder light just as easily in damp, wet weather as they do in dry weather. If, on the other hand, your tinder or wood is wet, they can be tricky to catch on fire. Plan on using numerous matches and loads of dry paper to get your fire started. As soon as you start a fire in wet weather, always keep a round of logs just inside your fire ring but not in your fire (never leave them unattended) until you break camp. This positioning will help dry them out.

In wet weather, you will not need to put your fire out completely at night if you properly bank it. To bank a fire, scatter the embers until the flames are gone and cover the fire pit with a light layer of dirt. To restart a banked fire, uncover the embers and bring them back together. Build your next fire on top of the embers. If you have practiced this, you may be able to get it to restart without a match by blowing on it.

Growing a fire

Once you have started you fire, the worst that can happen is it goes out. Each time you have to relight a fire, it wastes time, energy, and fuel. Campfires need to be constantly monitored. If the amount of wood left in the fire is smaller than a 4" log, it is time to add more.

Although you do not want your fire to go out, you also do not want it to grow out of control. You should never have more than two logs on the fire at a time – one that was on fire and one that is catching on fire. You also want the fire to stay in the center of your fire ring. And stray sticks or logs should be pushed back to the center with another thick stick.

Waterproofing your matches

The easiest way to waterproof your supplies to make sure they are in waterproof containers. This generally means plastic containers (or baggies) that seal. Waterproof match containers often have strike-plates on one or both ends, so you can use them with and stick-style match. You can further waterproof you matches by coating them in a thin layer of wax, but this will make them a little more difficult to light.

Fire paste

Fire paste is a small tube of chemicals that will light a fire in any weather. You place a small portion of it on top of a log and light it on fire. The fire will burn strongly enough to start even wet wood on fire, which reduces the amount of time and effort you will need to put into making a fire.

If you do not want to purchase fire paste, but prefer to make your own, the safest method is to coat or soak cotton balls in petroleum jelly. You can store these in sealed plastic bag. Then you would build your fire in an A-frame or bonfire style and use a cotton ball with the tinder, lighting the cotton ball first. There are also methods of making fire paste from gasoline, but these are not a good idea for BOB purposes.

Chapter 8: First Aid

Learning basic first aid

One of the biggest mistakes you could make when trying to help others who are injured is walking into a dangerous situation to help them. For example, you are walking down a street after an earthquake and hear cries coming from an unstable building. If you walk into the building to help, it may collapse on you, making another victim for professional rescuers to help.

Another thing you need to be careful about when it comes to first aid is learning it online or from books, without seeking professional certification in a hands-on class. Several websites and books on the market contain misinformation about lifesaving techniques. Even correct techniques, if performed improperly, can cause more harm than good. If you perform a lifesaving technique, such as CPR, on someone who does not need it, you can kill them

If you learn poor skills or learn from an unreliable source, you can endanger a person's life. For this reason, it is important to learn the skills from a certified instructor and demonstrate your ability.

The first step in survival preparation is to arm yourself with knowledge. Knowledge of CPR and first aid is readily available at your local Red Cross. This knowledge should be first on you list to learn because it can not only save your life, but it can save the life of those around you. Even children as young as 12 can take basic courses to help during disaster situations. Proper training for your family from the Red Cross will ensure you know the most up-to-date techniques to saved your loved ones in times of disaster.

Pre-packaged first aid kits

Stores have many first aid kits available in prepackaged sets. While purchasing these is a convenient option, it is not always the most economical. Frequently these kits are lacking in many important items. The benefit of purchasing a prepackaged kit is that they come in nice cases, and some of them are designed for backpackers – ideal for a BOB.

First aid containers

Containers for your first aid supplies should be flexible and soft. Zippered, nylon first aid bags are the best containers, but you could also use a zippered, plastic bag to store your needed supplies. Rigid containers are more difficult to pack and take up more space in your BOB. If you use your own container, make sure you mark it with the First Aid Cross so you can find it easier.

Although buying travel sized bottle of medicine for your BOB first aid kit is highly advised, never remove pills from the bottle in which they came and place them in a plastic baggie. It is always important to have the label information on any medicine you take. Read the label each time you take the medicine, and if you notice any side effects, bring the bottle to your physician.

Important kit contents

If you purchase a prepackaged first aid kit, check to make sure it contains all of the following items, or you can make your own first aid kit from scratch, by purchasing a portable bag and stocking it with:

- Sun block, lip balm, and bug spray
- Hydrogen peroxide, rubbing alcohol, iodine, and cotton balls
- Triple antibiotic ointment and petroleum jelly
- 5% Cortisone cream
- Tweezers, needles, safety pins, and a magnifying glass
- Calcium and salicylic based stomach medicine
- Loratidine and diphenhydramine based antihistamines
- Ibuprofen and acetaminophen
- Benzocaine toothache relief
- Anti-diarrheal medicine. laxatives, and antipurgatives
- Pseudoephedrine and guaifenesin cold remedies
- Variety of adhesive bandages and butterfly closures (at least two hundred)
- Gauze pads and first aid tape
- Sanitary napkins to stop major bleeding
- Four cloth slings and wood to make a splint
- Elastic bandage
- Hot and cold packs
- Disposable gloves
- Tongue depressors
- Small scissors and larger ones to cut away contaminated clothing
- Powdered electrolyte replacement

- Thermometer
- Small flashlight
- First aid manual

If you are unsure how to use these items or what they are, research them first. Always read the bottle of medication for the dosage information *every time you use it*. Do not buy over the counter medications that contain more than one active ingredient. If you mix these products with other products, you may overdose. Also, find out which medicines can and cannot be taken together. If you are using your BOB, chances are good that emergency care will be difficult to obtain. Do not do something that would make you need it.

First aid kits should contain a four-day supply of all the recommended medicines. It is important to know that medicines lose their effectiveness over time. Check the expiration dates on the medicines in your kit three or four times a year and replace what has expired. Ineffective medicines will weigh down your BOB without providing you with any benefit.

When stocking your first aid kit for your BOB, you need to consider the ages of those you will be traveling with to escape the disaster. Choose medications accordingly. Younger children can have little BOBs with first aid kits containing children's medicines. Toddlers require a chewable or liquid form of medicine while adults require concentrated pills to swallow.

Personalizing your first aid kit
Many people need prescription medicines on a daily basis. These medicines are more crucial to pack in a BOB first aid kit than any other medicines. However, the government regulates prescriptions. In order to get

three days worth of medicine for your BOB, you should renew your prescription three days early. This will give you the extra pills you may need in a disaster situation.

When disaster strikes, take not only your BOB, but also any medication you have remaining in your household. Like over-the-counter medicines, prescription medicine will lose effectiveness one year from the date they were filled. Whenever you renew your prescription, switch out your extra BOB supply with the fresh medicine and use the old pills before you use the rest of your refilled prescription.

EMT shears (trauma shears) and surgical shears
All first aid kits should contain some kind of scissors. The best kinds of scissors to use are trauma shears. Many emergency workers use these to cut away clothing and other obstructions, such as seat belts, when needed. They are extraordinarily strong and easy to use. They also have tips that are rounded to make it less likely you will cut the person.

While trauma shears are a good BOB first aid kit choice, a set of surgical shears is not. Most people do not have the training or ability to perform surgery under emergency situations. Surgical shears are only designed for the different needs associated with a surgery. Although trauma shears will not work well inside the body and surgical shears will, there is never a situation when an untrained person should attempt surgery.

The importance of ibuprofen (Advil), diphenhydramine (Benedryl), and anti-diarrheals
Ibuprofen (Advil) is a very important painkiller. It fights fever, and it can act as a blood thinner if needed. Unless

your doctor has told you not to use ibuprofen, it is relatively safe when used according to the package directions.

Diphenhydramine (Benedryl) is another important survival medicine. If you have an allergic reaction, diphenhydramine acts to reduce swelling. Those allergic to bee stings and other natural items should bring an epinephrine shot, as well, and keep it in their kit. Diphenhydramine also acts as a sedative.

When traveling the most common disease symptom people experience is diarrhea. Although diarrhea itself cannot kill you dehydration from having diarrhea can. Take an anti-diarrheal if you notice symptoms. Other ways of treating diarrhea are to drink more fluids, eat more frequently, and consume bananas, rice, applesauce, and toast or crackers. Purifying your water before drinking from unknown sources is a good preventative measure.

Chapter 9: Hygiene and Sanitation

Personal sanitation supplies

While water, shelter, and food are all high on the list of survival needs, sanitation and personal hygiene should be near the top of the list, too. Poor sanitary conditions and poor hygiene can lead to infection and disease. Because medical care is difficult to obtain in a disaster situation, it is even more important that you take care of yourself and your sanitation needs. Certain items in your BOB will help you take care of your sanitation needs while escaping disaster.

Here are some of the items you need from your BOB for sanitation:

- 3 gallons water
- First aid kit
- Iodine or chlorine water purification kits
- Package of sanitary items for women
- Three day supply of socks and underwear
- Mess kit, travel bottle of dish soap, and rag/bandana
- Hand sanitizer
- Toilet paper
- Travel toothbrush, dental floss or tape, and toothpaste
- Folding shovel and ax

- Antibacterial moist towelettes
- Antibacterial hand sanitizer (one bottle per person)
- Waterless shampoo
- Heavy duty plastic garbage bags
- Five-gallon bucket with tight lid
- Diapers and wet wipes are also important if you have a baby

Anti-bacterial soap vs. hand sanitizer

Anit-bacterial soap is not a good option for a BOB. It requires water to use in order to rinse it away, and it can pose environmental problems. An environment that is recovering from a disaster will already be stressed and trying to purge contaminants from it. You do not need to contribute to the damage.

Hand sanitizer is a good alternative to antibacterial soap. Not only will it keep your hands clean, but also, it leaves not residue or environmental footprint. It conserves water by evaporating quickly and eliminating the need to rinse. The negative side of hand sanitizer is that is can make your hands dry and cracked. If you are traveling with hand sanitizer, you may want to consider rubbing a little petroleum jelly into your hands at night before you go to bed.

Toilet paper

Although it is possible to live without toilet paper by using leaves, corncobs, and other items to wipe, toilet paper is a nice luxury to have in a survival situation. Toilet paper provides a germ barrier between your hand and your waste that helps you remain healthy.

Toilet paper is relatively compact – especially if you purchase the basic roll – and it is lightweight. If you pack a roll, it can be used for multiple things, such as blowing your nose or wiping out a dirty pot.

It is important when going to the bathroom to dig a pit about 3-feet deep and cover it when you are finished. Nobody wants accidentally to step in someone's waste. Human waste is also notorious for spreading disease. Covering it will prevent it from contaminating the area.

Sunscreen

If a disaster occurs, you may have to walk for three days. Three days in the sun without the protection of sunscreen can cause painful, blistering, sunburns. It is extremely important that you do not forget to pack your sunscreen in your BOB. It is equally essential to remember to put it on in the morning and once every four hours. If you find that you get wet, you will need to reapply your sunscreen even if it is waterproof.

The best sunblock is SPF15 or SPF30. When you are walking in the sun for three days, your goal is not to get a tan, but to protect your skin completely. Some people need more protection than others, so you need to be honest with yourself about which of these would work best for you. Again, this is something you can confirm before a disaster strikes. Plan a three-day weekend at the beach. Use the sunblock you feel will be the best and see if it prevents you from getting even a little pink.

Another important note is that sunscreen will allow rays of sunlight through while sunblock usually uses nanotechnology to prevent the sun from penetrating your skin. Sunblock is a better choice for a BOB.

Hand wipes and microfiber towels

When you are fleeing a disaster area, you may not have the time or water to wash your hands as frequently as you should wash them. Carrying hand wipes or baby wipes will make the process of cleansing your hands quick and efficient without creating a time or water issue.

Microfiber towels are designed to be superabsorbent. If you pack one or two of these, they will help you clean up any spills and dry and wet items without becoming soaked.

Dental care

When faced with a disaster where you are fleeing the area, you may not be concerned about your teeth. However, there is no reason why you should not take care of one of your valuable assets. If you neglect your teeth, you cannot only cause dental disease, you can also contribute to future dental problems that will give you a constant negative future reminder of the disaster you survived.

Toothbrushes, toothpaste, and dental floss or tape are all lightweight and take up little space in your BOB. At a minimum, you should brush in the morning after eating and at night before going to bed.

If you do not have some of your dental care items, you can make substitutions. If you do not have a toothbrush, you can use a twig or your finger. If you do not have toothpaste, you can use baking soda or even plain water. Toothpicks are a decent substitute for dental floss/ tape. Many multiblade knives also have toothpicks as well.

If you are prone to having toothaches or losing fillings, you may want to pack an emergency dental repair kit in your BOB. These kits are easy to use and will get you through until you can find an available dentist.

Mirrors

Mirrors are multipurpose tools that can help you survive a disaster in several ways. You can use mirrors for signalling by reflecting the light of the sun onto the object you want to signal. You can use mirrors to check cuts and injuries you cannot see. Mirrors can help you see around corners and in tight spots you might not normally be able to view. Finally, in a pinch, mirrors can concentrate the rays of the sun and help you start a fire.

When purchasing a mirror for your BOB bag, you may want something small and manageable. It is also very important that your BOB mirror is not breakable.

Feminine needs

Women always should prepare their BOB for the heaviest time of their cycle. Although rags, bandanas, old washcloths, and even some leaves like lamb's ear (not poison ivy, poison oak, or poison sumac) can be used, having feminine napkins is the best way to keep your clothes clean and prevent embarrassing accidents.

If it happens to be that time of your cycle when a disaster strikes, be sure to take extra breaks to drink water and change your feminine protection. You also may want to consider packing a multivitamin in your BOB first aid kit and take it every day. If you do not, you may become anemic and tired, which will make travel much slower than what it needs to be.

Chapter 10: Important BOB Tools

Hammer or mallet

If you are planning to set up a tent or tarp for shelter, you will need either a hammer or a mallet to pound the stakes into the ground. Hammers are heavier to carry than mallets. Although they can double as a weapon or can break thick ice to open a hole to the water underneath in times of need, they are sometimes too powerful for driving tent stakes into the ground. The do have a claw on the back to help pull tent stakes out of the ground. In addition, they will take up less space in your pack or can be hung from the outside of it.

Mallets are lighter in weight but more bulky to carry. A mallet gives you more control over how hard you are hitting an item, but it will not provide as much force when you are using it. The head of the mallet is made from rubber or plastic and so it will not dent or damage metal. However, this can be a negative as well as a positive in a disaster situation.

Survival knives

Knives have three basic styles, folding, sliding, and fixed blade. The folding knife is designed to fit in your pocket, so the handle and blade are connected with a pivot. You do not need to purchase a case for it, and it will frequently come with multiple blades. The problem with these knives is that they are weak at the joint where they fold. This means that they are prone to breaking and are not capable of heavy-duty cutting. They also need a method of locking the blade open so that it does not accidentally slip closed in use and cut the user. There are many types of locking mechanisms. The simplest and most widely used is the slip joint, which is not really a lock and closes when you put enough pressure on it. Be sure you know how to use the locking mechanism if you have a folding knife in your BOB.

Knives with fixed blades must be carried in a case or sheath. They do not fold, so the blade is always out and unprotected unless you cover it. These come in varying degrees of quality, but are usually stronger than folding knives because the blade is rooted in the handle. You do not have to worry that this type of knife will accidentally fold down when you are using it.

A sliding knife requires the user to press a switch extending the blade from the handle. A utility knife is and example of this kind of knife. Some people prefer utility knives because the blade can be changed. However, the blade is not very strong, and sometimes has breakaway points where it will break off, so a new, sharper surface is presented. Utility knives are not practical for survival.

Machete
Unless you live in a jungle with much overgrowth, a machete is not a necessity for traveling with your BOB. When selecting knives, some people believe that bigger is better. Instead, people should look for the right type of knife to meet their needs. Machetes are designed to hack through rough underbrush, they really have no

other purpose other than to defend yourself, but any knife can provide you with some protection.

If you are interested in purchasing a knife that does not fold, try the knife that the military issues to Air Force personnel. This knife is strong and solid but comes in a more manageable size.

Choosing a survival knife

There are several styles of knives to choose from and several prominent knife manufacturers. The best tools to place in your BOB are those that have more than one function. Thus, it makes sense that a knife with more than one function would be the best knife to choose. However, you also need a reliable tool, that will not fail you, and protection alone is a secondary feature of any knife.

The best way to decide which knife is best for you is to go to the store and examine several of them. Decide whether you want something that will fold in your pocket or whether you want something that will rest on your side. Finding a folding knife with a saw option can help you cut branches to support your tarp, if needed. Finding a knife with a fixed blade that will help you clean fish is also a good option.

Duct tape

Duct tape is a strong tape that is also waterproof. It is sticky, flexible, and resists weather. Often, people back the claim that you can survive anything with duct tape. If your shoes break, you can make new ones with duct tape. If you need a hat, you can make one from duct tape. If you are looking for a bucket, again, duct tape will help you. Although all of these items take time to build, the meaning is clear. With imagination and duct tape, you can build anything you may be lacking. Duct tape is also good for making repairs. Although you should carry special kits for repairing air mattresses, duct tape can repair everything else, from clothing to tents.

Garbage bags

Although you are hiking away from a disaster area, you should still keep your trash to yourself. For food wrappers, you need to keep them in a sealed plastic baggie. One should be enough to keep all your trash inside.

You can also pack a garbage bag – not for trash but to use as an emergency raincoat for your pack. Cut holes for the straps and then use duct tape to ensure it stays in place. Garbage bags used for this purpose need to be at least .8 mils thick for durability. Do not assemble it until you need it (right before it starts to rain) because it will make getting in and out of your pack more difficult.

Multi-tool

These tools can be useful if you choose a fixed blade knife instead of a folding one with multiple tool options. Frequently, these will also come with a small folding blade that will be useful in situations that required more delicate work than what you can practically do with your larger fixed blade. They tend to fold into neat packets and come with pliers, which most folding knives do not offer. However, if you already have a multi-use, folding knife you should not add this weight to your BOB bag.

Light weight shovel

The best shovel for your BOB is a survival shovel or entrenching shovel. These are small and will fold into an easy to carry pouch. They are also extremely lightweight. Their edge is sharp enough to break through the grass and help you form your fire pit.

Camp axe

If you are using a tarp for shelter, a camp ax is vital. It is also useful to chop firewood if you are using a traditional campfire to keep you warm or to cook your food. Axes made specially for camping are often called hatchets.

Axes can be one-sided or two-sided; you need one that has the blade on only one side for survival purposes. You also need an axe with a sheath over the blade to keep it from cutting when it is not being used. It is also best to find one that is not fitted onto a wooden handle but is instead one piece.

Cutting wood with an axe is another skill that should be practiced before you need it. You should not swing the axe straight up and down in your attempt to cut, but it should hit the wood at angles to remove chunks.

Chapter 11: A Light for the Road

Lighting options

There are many flashlights, headlamps, and lanterns available to meet your needs for portable light. As with anything, sometimes there are several good choices that depend on personal preference.

The lighting choice you make for your BOB should be durable. You do not want it to break when you need it most. It should also be long-lasting, lightweight, and easy to use. If it uses batteries, be sure to rotate them with fresh ones a few times a year. Even batteries that have not been used can go bad after a couple years.

Emergency flashlights

One of the best ways to have light as you are escaping a disaster is a crank flashlight. These do not require batteries but generate about an hour's worth of light after a few minutes of cranking. Some of these also come with sockets for charging cell phones. While cranking can seem a tedious way of obtaining light, you will not need to worry about dead batteries.

Battery operated flashlights are another option for providing light when it is dark. These require no priming and deliver light instantly. However, their battery life limits them. Since a BOB is a kit, which you use only during times of disaster, you need to make sure you are replacing old BOB batteries with new ones regularly.

The longest-life batteries are those that are rechargeable. These batteries are made for environmental reasons, but they work better than regular batteries and are worth the extra cost. You can place them on the charger every few months to ensure they have not lost their charge. If you use rechargeable batteries, make sure the set you use is all of the same type. Also, eventually these batteries age and become less useful as well. Always label your batteries with a permanent marker to record the date of purchase so you can see when they are getting old.

Alternate sources of light

You will find many light sources in the camping section of any store. The most common (aside from flashlights) is a lantern. Lanterns have been a camping staple for years, but they do not provide reliable light for the person who is escaping a disaster situation.

Lanterns require you to carry liquid fuel (unless they are lantern shaped flashlights), and they are bulky to fit in your BOB. Liquid fuel can always spill and not only ruin the rest of the items in your bag but also make them flammable. Storing fuel is a difficult matter, so it is best to ignore lanterns when packing your BOB. Even lantern shaped flashlights should be avoided because they take up more space than is necessary.

One alternate source of light you might want to consider if you have children is glowsticks. Glow sticks do little in the way of illumination on a dark night, but they can provide a source of comfort for your little ones. Three glowsticks are relatively lightweight and will provide more than enough luminescence for three nights on the road.

LED headlamps

LED headlamps are small and bright. Because they fit on your head, they allow your hands to be free for doing other things. They use less of their battery power per hour and the bulbs themselves rarely go bad. You can purchase lamps that have spotlight (one beam of concentrated light for seeing in a straight line) and floodlight (a beam of light that is not as intense but allows you to see a wider area) capabilities.

The biggest difficulty when using a headlamp is walking at night. Although you should make your camp before it gets dark, there may be times when you are forced to walk in the dark, such as when safety is a concern, or when you have not found a suitable place to make camp. At night, a headlamp illuminates the area in front of you, but not the ground. If there are obstacles (and there probably will be many of these after a disaster), you will not see them and may hurt yourself. As a backup measure, you may wish to carry a regular flashlight as well. The combination of flashlight and headlamp will give you the best illumination for night walking.

LED key chain lights

If you have no other source of light, an LED key chain can be a lifesaver. Like space blankets, these are not practical for standard use, but they are more valuable than the flimsy, metallic blankets. These do not cast a wide beam or even a strong beam, but they will help in a pinch. Try to find one that does not make you constantly hold a button in order to keep it lit.

Candles

The only candles worth bringing in a BOB are a couple of small citronella candles to keep bugs away. Bugs can be difficult to deal with in some areas, especially at night. Citronella candles do a good job of keeping them away from you while you cook a meal.

Although you can use a candle to light a campfire, it is better for you to light a small piece of tinder and light the fire that way.

Chapter 12: Communicating

Cell phones

Cell phones are a common method of portable communication across the distances. They can be very valuable during any disaster. Cell phones with texting capabilities can often use text to get through to others when the regular phones are filled with calls from concerned family members. However, cell phones are also prone to losing their battery power or signal at the worst times. Cell phones are a good back up method of communication, but if you are planning on using one in your BOB, you may want to consider carrying a hand crank flashlight with a cell phone charging option. In addition, do not plan emergency routes that will take you through a deep canyon (never a good idea anyway) or a forest that is especially dense.

Maintaining an emergency contact

Every person should have an emergency contact network. Disasters can affect large areas and frequently they shut down lines of communication making it difficult to notify all of your loved ones of your status. Having an emergency contact in place, whom you have established as a call person to coordinate emergency communication is important. This person should live out-of-state and should be willing to contact others on your behalf. You should check in with your main, emergency contact once per day and update him or her on your status and your plans for the next twenty-four hours. This person can then relay the information on to other family and friends. They can also tell you of important news updates to keep you informed of events in the area you are escaping.

Emergency radio

A small, hand crank radio is an effective way to follow news updates. The benefit of a hand crank radio is that it does not require batteries, so you do not have to worry about it running out of power. However, because the market has recently been flooded with these radios, some are not very durable and have been assembled poorly. Do research before purchasing one. Some hand crank radios also have a power insert to recharge cell phones, which makes them doubly useful.

MP3 players are also valuable if you are careful and only listen to them occasionally throughout the day to conserve their battery power. The down side is that one person will have to listen to the news and then share it if traveling in a group. It is not a good idea to have all members of your group with earphones on at the same time, in case there is an audible warning of danger.

Signaling tools

If you have to travel through a disaster zone, there may be rescue workers around who are looking for survivors they can aid. There are several ways you can attract the attention of rescue workers. Frequently they will be flying overhead, and so you will need to signal an airplane or helicopter. Keep in mind, if you want help, you will need to be near a place the help can land. Roads and open, flat fields away from power lines are the best places to land traditional helicopters and airplanes. If they are equipped with pontoons because you are in a place near water, they will be able to land on the water, as well.

One of the traditional methods of signaling is with a mirror. In order to use a signal mirror, you hold the reflective part so that it is facing the sun. Hold your hand in between the mirror and the approaching airplane. Move the mirror until you see the sun's reflection on your hand. Then, flick the mirror up and down to attract the plane's attention. If you do not have a mirror, any reflective surface, such as a knife blade, clean pan, or even left over aluminum foil can work as signaling devices.

Another method of signaling you need help is to build three campfires in a triangle formation, or you can add wet vegetation to any campfire to create an attention-grabbing column of smoke.

Another important way of signaling distress is through a whistle. If you become disoriented and lost or if you are injured and cannot proceed, you can easily lose your voice trying to call for help. A whistle allows you to signal others and conserve your voice.

Flares also provide intense burning signals, which you can hold in your hand and wave to attract attention. Flares come in large sizes that burn longer and small multi-packs. For a BOB, the smaller multi-packs are a way to ensure you do not have only one chance to attract attention without adding excess weight. Flares are dangerous and burn very hot. They can catch surrounding vegetation on fire, which will create its own disaster situation. Be careful when using flares.

Flashing LED strobe lights are a safer alternative to flares. These are not as visible on sunny, clear days, but they will not catch their surroundings on fire.

Watches
The minimum features on a BOB watch should be the ability to tell time accurately, an alarm, and the ability to accurately keep track of days. When traveling, especially if you are hiking out of a disaster zone, you will need to take breaks. A watch with an alarm can be set to remind you when it is time to get started again. Breaks can determine the difference between achieving your mileage goal and falling far short. Sometimes, when under duress, people can fall asleep for long periods of time and wake up thinking they only took a brief nap. Your watch will tell you what time it is, so you can adjust your day accordingly and are not surprised when night falls.

Additional features of a BOB watch that can be useful but are not required are a thermometer, barometer, and altimeter. The thermometer will let you know what the temperature is, so you will not be surprised if you sit down and become rapidly cold. A barometer can warn you of incoming storms, and an altimeter can let you know if you need to boil your water a little longer to purify it.

The compass
There are several types of compasses; two are the most useful for traveling with a BOB. The first kind comes with a flip lid that contains a site line (the liquid-filled lensatic or military compass). The second is a thin, flat rectangle made of clear plastic and designed to lie on a map as you plot your direction (a liquid filled orienteering or protractor compass.

These compasses can be tied on a string around your neck to keep them near at hand and encourage frequent use. It is a well-known fact that people who travel through the wilderness without a compass will end up going in a circle. Never rely on your own sense of direction to guide you. Even familiar surroundings can look unfamiliar after a disaster strikes.

Using a compass is as difficult as using a map. There are many courses available that will teach you to use each. You should enroll in one before the need arises to use these skills.

Some people may be tempted to replace their compass with a GPS. The problem is that GPS has the similar limitations of a cell phone. When you need constant directional information for three days, your GPS will eventually run out of batteries. If you turn it off to conserve battery power, you could get off track and end up costing yourself hours of time.

Reading a map
Many people take maps for granted and believe they will be able to read one when the time comes. Other people just try to avoid them altogether. It is a good idea to learn how to read a map. Both topographic and planimetric maps are good for planning an escape route. Planimetric maps are the standard maps that we have the most familiarity with using. Road maps, which do not generally have elevations marked, are an example of a planimetric map.

If you are serious about plotting a safe evacuation route over unfamiliar ground, you will learn to read a topographic map and use one of these to plot your route. Topographic maps are filled with a series of elevation lines that give you a detailed view of the landscape if you know how to use them. They are very important if you will need to travel across areas you have never traveled through. However, it is always a good to explore as much of your evacuation route as you can in advance.

Whichever map you choose, mark your evacuation route, and then have the map laminated so that you can fold it. There are also special waterproofing products made for maps. If you do not have your map protected, the elements can destroy it or erase your plotted route before you arrive at your destination. It is also a good idea to share a copy of your evacuation route with your out-of-state contact.

Chapter 13: Money and Documents

Important Documents

Many of the important documents you will need to take in your BOB (or at least have a copy of the official record) are items you will find in your wallet. The other documents should be sealed in a plastic zippered bag and placed in a side pocket of your Bug Out Bag. These documents include:

- Driver's licenses
- Credit cards and insurance cards
- Emergency contact information
- Medical information
- Weapon's permits
- Evacuation map
- Insurance policies
- Birth certificates/death certificates/adoption papers
- Immunization records
- Portable first aid information booklet
- Pocket survival reference
- Recent pay stub and resume
- Professional licenses
- Passports and Social Security cards
- Recent high-quality photos of family members
- Marriage license

Cash and wallet

Although coins are heavy to carry, in a disaster situation, you may find change hard to find. For this reason, it is a good idea to have enough change on you, so you always can pay the exact amount. As metal, coins also have some value beyond denominational worth. Coins are also good if you are using a vehicle to evacuate and need to pay tolls. Be sure to carry a roll of pennies, dimes, nickels, and quarters, and $20 in dollar coins. In addition to coins, you need cash on hand. Be sure to carry $20 in ones and $40 in fives in your BOB wallet.

The wallet you keep stocked in your BOB should be waterproof. This will keep the items safe from damaging moisture and inclement weather. When you are ready to evacuate, your BOB wallet will be pre-stocked and ready to go. It can contain some of those important documents you normally do not carry in your wallet but may be necessary when fleeing a disaster. Although you should keep your BOB wallet in a side pocket of your BOB, you should also take the wallet you normally use with you when you evacuate as well.

Passport

A passport is an important document that confirms your identity. Even if you never leave the country, applying for and keeping current a passport is a good idea. In a disaster situation, it is even more vital.

Should you need to leave the country after a disaster, it normally takes six to eight weeks to apply for and receive a passport. Even expedited passports will not arrive immediately. If you have a passport and need to leave, it is as simple as walking to an airport and booking a flight.

If you need to apply for a job after relocating, a passport is the only document you need to establish your identification.

Writing materials

When you are experiencing a disaster, writing can be a good way to clear your mind and thoughts. You can even express your anger with your traveling partners on paper (without showing it to them) and relieve pent up frustration while maintaining peace throughout the camp.

Personal contact information

All of your personal contact information should be stored separately from your official documents in another sealed plastic zipper baggie. This information does not need to be accessed easily and can be placed in the bottom of your BOB. However, you need to have all this information available and up-to-date. Here is the information you need on your personal contact sheet:

- Your name, address, and phone number.
- The name, address, and phone number(s) of two or three emergency contacts.
- The name, telephone, fax, and business address of your family physician.
- Your passport number with its place of issue and date of issue.
- Your insurance providers (medical, home, life, and car), their contact information, and your policy number.

- The name, address, telephone, website, and account numbers for your personal bank(s) and investing firm(s).
- The name, credit card number, website, and phone number(s) of your credit cards.
- A list of your computer accounts.
- Vehicle identification numbers, year, make, and model of all vehicles.
- Firearm serial numbers, makes, and models.
- Lawyer name, address, phone number, and fax.

Chapter 14: Surviving with Pets

Pet BOB

If you have pets, you should try to take them with you when you evacuate a disaster situation. They sell pet backpacks that work as ideal BOB containers. Pets need special things to take with them when you are evacuating. Here are the items you should pack for them:

- Pet food (for three days)
- Non-spill, lightweight bowls for food and water
- Potable water for your pet (You will need about 1.5 gallons, so you may have to put some of this in your bag.)
- Sturdy leashes and or harnesses, and muzzles
- Can opener and plastic zipper bag if you pet uses canned food
- Any pet medications (three day supply)
- Rope and stake to tie animals while traveling

You will need to rotate your pet food as frequently as you rotate your human food. If you use dry pet food, you should put the amount needed for three days in plastic zipper baggies. You need to make sure that your pet has the same type of food in their BOB as what they eat every day. Although it can be tempting to substitute heavy canned food for lightweight dry food, changing food can add to a pet's distress and cause your pet to stop eating.

Also, your pet will need to practice wearing his BOB. It may be best to begin with the BOB unloaded. Once the pet adjusts to carrying a pack, you can slowly add more weight until it is full.

Collapsible carriers

Although collapsible carriers may seem ideal for transporting your pet out of a disaster area, some can be quite bulky and should only be used if you are able to evacuate in a vehicle. The one exception is purse-style pet carriers for small and exotic pets. If your pet is small, you can decide whether or not to carry it. If your pet is exotic, you will probably need to carry it. In this case, you also will have to carry the pet's BOB or have someone traveling with you shoulder the extra burden.

Pet mess kits

There are several collapsible bowls you can use for your pet's food and water needs. There are also food and water travel kits, which allow you to carry food and water and serve them in a compact kit. You can also purchase round, disposable, plastic food dishes with lids for on the go pet dishes.

Animal safety

You can find pet first aid kits that will help with any pet emergency. Most pet first aid kits contain gauze pads, hydrogen peroxide, antiseptic/alcohol wipes, scissors, exam gloves, gauze roll bandages, tweezers, pet first aid book, saline solution/ eye wash., first aid ointment, iodine, hydrocortisone cream, pill gun, and cold packs. Keep in mind that different pets may have different needs. Like humans, pets should have a three-day's supply of medicines if they take them on a regular basis. Rotate these as you would rotate human medicines.

If you live in a cold area, you may want to include a pet coat and pet boots for your animal. There are also boots designed to travel over rough ground.

Keeping your pet from wandering away

When evacuating an animal, you should use a harness or collar and leash if you animal is walking with you. A muzzle is also a necessary tool. Animals under stressful situations are prone to bite, even if they are normally very friendly. Putting a muzzle on your pet will prevent it from biting someone out of nervousness and causing a wound that may need medical attention or slow your evacuation down. Never approach an unknown animal when you are fleeing a disaster. All animals will bite if provoke and many will become disoriented after certain disasters.

Portable pet playpens are not practical unless you are able to use your vehicle to evacuate. Instead, plan on using a tent and keeping you pet inside at night, while using a leash that has been staked into the ground during the day when you are stopped.

72-hours worth of food and water

A three-day supply of water is about 1-½ gallons for most animals. If you have water sources along your evacuation route, you will be able to refill after purifying the water, but you always should pack enough water for the entire time. During a disaster, the water source may become inaccessible. It is best to purify water using only the boiling method when you are planning on giving it to your pet. Animals have different tolerances for chemical means of purification.

As a pet owner, you are the best judge as to how much and how frequently you will need to feed your pet. If your pet is normally more lethargic, you may want to pack 1/3 more food for each day to ensure it does not go hungry after extending more energy.

The importance of vaccinations

Vaccines for pets are relatively low-cost and life saving. Many pet vaccines are to keep you pet from developing life-threatening, serious diseases. A few will protect you and your family as well. The number of humans catching rabies after being bit by a dog has become non-existent in countries, which require the widespread use of the rabies vaccine in pets. However, bats and other wild animals still carry the virus. Protect you pet and yourself with this simple preventative measure. Keep a record of your pet's vaccinations and emergency contact information in a sealed, plastic, zipper bag inside your pet's BOB. Keeping a picture of your pet in your wallet will also help if your pet should become separated from you.

Chapter 15: Self-defense

Camouflage and secure sleeping

Under most circumstances, escaping a disaster will be relatively easy with few dangers. However, there are times when looters and gangs scavenge through disaster areas for goods to steal. One way to defend yourself from unwanted visitors is to use camouflage.

When you are moving, camouflage does not work as well as when you are still. However, when you have set up camp, and you are sleeping at night, it is a likely time for a thief to steal your gear. To hide your camp, be careful and burn your fire for limited time; also, speak quietly with others, unless you are lost or in need of attention.

The quickest and lightest way to camouflage your sleeping area is to use natural underbrush to cover it. Covering a bivy sack to hide it is easier than covering a full tent. There are also camouflage covers you can use to cover larger items. There are even covers that will make your tent completely invisible in any terrain. However, when you use these, you will be blind to the world around you.

If you select a tent cover for your BOB, it is best to store it in your optional bag. While camouflage is a good option in some cases, in others you may not need it.

Another helpful item to purchase is a tent lock. These are small locks that fit on the zippers of your tent to secure them. If you can hike or drive to a place where there is a campground, this can provide added security while you sleep. There may even be a security guard on patrol.

Fighting without a weapon

For those who do not like to carry weapons, there are many methods available to protect yourself and your family. In fact, not everyone is capable of using a firearm or lethal weapon. *Threatening* looters is not an effective method of protection. Anything you threaten – from pepper spray to shooting – needs to be swiftly backed up by action if potential looters step out of line. People who only use weapons to threaten may soon find the weapons they once carried used against them. Some form of self-defense to rely on is necessary in all circumstances.

Pepper spray and non-lethal weapons

Even if you prefer to carry a weapon for safety, a key chain with pepper spray (capsicum spray) is a good, non-lethal stand-by. Pepper spray works well against humans and animals by temporarily blinding the attacker (for up to 45 minutes). It is also easy to aim. When searching for a good pepper spray, it should contain a CRC rating of grater than 1%.

Another important survival skill you and your family need is a course in self-defense. Hand-to-hand combat and martial arts skills help keep you and your family from becoming victims of unwanted aggression. These skills should be seen as a minimum investment in protection. Self-defense classes are easy to find, and many communities have several options.

Lethal weapons and ammunition

Using a lethal weapon is a matter of choice for the BOB. When you remain in your home, with a stockpile of supplies, lethal weapons are an almost necessary defense against looters; however, if you are fleeing an area during or immediately after a disaster, your need for lethal means to defend yourself drops. In fact, as you flee a disaster area, those fleeing with you are frequently going to be those with the same "flight" instinct. Although non-lethal means of defense are the best to pack in your BOB, some people may not feel secure without a lethal weapon.

No matter what your weapon of choice, in order to defend yourself properly and avoid unfortunate (and potentially deadly) accidents, you and your family will need proper training in how to use the weapon. Unlike non-lethal methods of defense, lethal weapons cause immediate damage. That is why everyone should know how to use it safely. You also need to practice using the weapon, so you do not have to try to remember how to use it when the need arises. Even children need to be educated in the proper use of your weapons. Although it is more difficult to restrict access to weapons in a BOB, children should never be allowed to access the weapons without adult supervision.

Choosing a weapon with a lock or lockable case is important, but it is difficult to find weapons that will fit in a lockable case, which in turn fits into your BOB without revealing that you are carrying it. Unless you are traveling through a dangerous area, your lethal weapon should be in its locked case at all times. Failure to secure your firearm can result in not only losing it or getting it jammed with dirt and grime, but also death of a family member because the weapon accidentally

discharges.

Shotguns are the easiest firearm to use, but not practical for a BOB because of its size. The shot scatters in a wide spray, which makes it easier to hit your target than if you are shooting one bullet. Most shotguns only have about six shots before needing to be reloaded. Rifles and handguns, require you to have better accuracy in order to hit your target, but you are given more shots before you need to reload. Rifles are also difficult to conceal in a BOB, but most handguns are not. On the flip side, some people have difficulty hunting with a handgun (always an optional way to supplement your food supply when you carry a lethal means of defense). Having another method of obtaining food is always an added benefit.

Knives are lethal weapons you already need to carry with your BOB. If you want to obtain training in fighting with a knife, it can be of benefit. However, fighting with a knife is a difficult skill to learn.

Bows and crossbows only have one shot. These weapons are not for beginners and also are difficult to pack in a BOB. Also tasers, swords, and martial arts weapons are not for beginners and difficult to pack. None of these should not be purchased only to defend your family while escaping disaster.

Chapter 16: Extras for Your Optional Bag

Sewing kit

To make your own survival sewing kit, take a matchbox (with no matches in it) and glue a magnetic strip on the inside of it. Place two or three needles, a two small, two medium, and two large safety pins in the box. Add several buttons of different sizes.

Close the box. Around the outside, wrap white, black, off-white, gray, and red thread in rows. Lay a piece of thread tape across the ends of thread or cut small slits in the side of the box to clasp the thread.

Parachute cord (550 cord) or 50' nylon rope

Parachute cord was initially used for the military. It is lightweight and durable. It also has the unique ability to breakdown into smaller ropes – even all the way down to fishing line or sewing thread. Because of its unique versatility, it is the ultimate survival rope.

Despite its military origins, parachute cord is widely available to civilians. When purchasing the commercially available cords, you may want to be sure the cord has at least seven inner strands and is made entirely of nylon. Some commercial products marketed as "parachute cord" use fiberfill instead of inner cords, making the rope much weaker.

For the survivalist, special "survival bracelets" are made from a few feet of parachute cord. In an emergency, these can be unwound and used. If you use parachute cord and need to cut it, you will have to heat the end by holding it near a flame or heat source. Then you will need to crimp it closed with pliers or even by pressing it between two rocks. This will prevent the cord from unraveling.

Rope can always benefit a BOB, but if you are using a tarp, you will need at least 50'. When you practice setting up your tarp, you can determine the lengths and number of pieces of rope you will need. Include these in your BOB.

N95 face mask

Under certain disaster situations, it may be vital to wear a N95, N99, or N100 face mask while escaping. These masks filter the air you breathe from radiation, chemical, and biological weapons. They also filter disease from pandemic infested air.

These face masks are labeled based on the percentage of pathogens they filter from the air around you. An N95 filters 95% of the pathogens, an N99 filters 99%, and an N100 filters 99.9% of all biological pathogens. Any of these masks are good to stock near your BOB.

It is essential to know if your mask is for a one-time use or for reuse. Never reuse a mask only designed to be used once. If you suspect you have come in contact with a pathogen from a biological weapon that has been dispersed in your area, you should remove your clothing and shower in hot water before evacuating in clean, unexposed clothing. You should also visit a physician as soon as possible to receive recommended treatment. Be sure to inform him or her of your exposure, the time, and the measures you took to prevent further infection. Other members of your family or BOB traveling companions should also shower if contaminated before escaping.

If you have a N95 or better face mask and you experience a disaster that is not biological, chemical, radiation, or pandemic related, you might want to place the face mask in your optional bag or leave it behind. It will add weight that may not be necessary unless you are likely to encounter impure air conditions.

Binoculars

When traveling away from a disaster, being able to see what is happening in front of you at a distance can help you plan your route of escape better. Binoculars are excellent tools for seeing at distances.

Binoculars for your BOB should be lightweight and compact. However, you want to have binoculars that are powerful for their size. The larger the magnification, the further you will be able to see. However, as magnification increases, your field of view will decrease. The second number you will find on binoculars is the objective diameter. This number will tell you how bright the objects will be when you view them. For example, if one binocular set is labeled 3X50 and the other is labeled 6x25, the first one will give you a brighter view and the second one will let you see things that are further away from you.

Inspirational items

Everyone has items that are special to him or her and have a high emotional value. Some examples are photos, special items of jewelry, a figurine, or even a travel drive with important business files. Small items that are dear to you are fine to pack in your optional bag after all your needs have been taken care of.

Some people also have spiritual items, such as Bibles, that comfort them in times of need. In any disaster, you should try to keep these items with you to help keep your morale high. Traveling from one point to the next in a disaster situation can be stressful and at times you may feel like giving up on everything. Having items that provide you with hope will help keep you moving forward to your goal.

The optional bag is something for you to take on your escape that does not contain life-giving items. These items may need to be abandoned along the way if you must travel on foot and need to remove some weight from your load. However, if you are capable of bringing them the entire way, they will give you something to cling to that has not been lost.

Chapter 17: Organizing and Maintaining Your BOB

How to pack your bug-out bag

Packing your BOB correctly will reduce the amount of fatigue you feel after a long day of carrying it on your back. In general, you want the heaviest items close to your back and toward the middle or top. You also want to have items you may need frequently, such as maps, or items you may need quickly, such as emergency supplies, in outer, easy-to-access pockets. For comfort, softer items may need to be placed near your back, or you can slip your sleeping pad in to pad your back and provide comfort.

If you have difficulty packing your BOB and run out of room, reassess what you are taking and what containers you are using. If you have tried to pack a full-sized tube of toothpaste, you should purchase a travel-sized toothpaste. Make sure you have transferred boxed foods into plastic zipper baggies.

Compartmentalization

One of the keys to a successfully packed BOB is compartmentalization. If your BOB does not come with numerous compartments, you will not be able to organize it well. You will also have to unpack everything before you are able to get anything out that you need.

Compartmentalization allows you to pack you items in a logical way and maintain your access to them. Internally your pack should have one main compartment. Externally, your pack should have at least six to ten different compartments for your items.

Pack organization

If you have purchased a standard backpacking-style backpack with one main compartment with at least six minor compartments, here is a sample of how you should pack:

Main compartment: your tent and water should be placed vertically and to one side. Your camping utensils, fuel tablets, and cook stove should be on the bottom of the other side. You can place all your food on top of that. And place important documents down one side. Fill in the empty spaces with clean clothes and underwear.

Underneath your main compartment, should be a compartment or space for you sleeping bag and sleeping pad. If your BOB has a smaller compartment on this section, you can store your rain gear in it.

The top pocket of your BOB should contain maps, notebooks, writing instruments, and outer layers you have removed to keep yourself comfortable.

You can keep the food for your next lunch and any fuel you may need for it in one of the outside pockets for easy access along with your filled canteen or main water container. You can also keep many of your minor supplies, such as your light source, tent stakes, shovel, weapons, and first aid kit. Be sure to organize each outside pouch so that it contains items you would use together.

Waterproofing your pack and tent

You can never tell what kind of weather you will have when you need to escape a disaster. Most BOBs are made with breathable material that you will need to cover in extreme rainstorms to prevent the contents from becoming drenched. Even if your BOB says it is waterproof, it is always a good idea to double the protection by covering it. Although your important documents, first aid kit, food, campfire and camp stove supplies, maps, and other important items should be secured in plastic zipper baggies, you should do your best to protect your items as a whole.

You can begin by waterproofing the inside of your BOG before you pack it by lining it with a plastic trash bag. This will ensure water does not seep in from the sides. If you are able, when you finish packing the BOB, secure the top of the bag closed with a twist tie.

On the exterior of the BOB, you should use a tarp, rain poncho, or plastic trash bag to protect it. These should not be placed over the BOB unless/ until it starts to rain. Keep in mind that you will need a rain poncho or some wet weather gear for yourself. Also, if you are not careful how you combine your rain gear with that of your BOBs, you may end up creating a stream of water that flows from your neck down to your back.

Pack storage and maintenance

When you check your BOB for routine maintenance, make sure all the zippers are working. Also, examine the stitching to see if any of it looks worn out or is beginning to fray. You should practice hiking in your BOB occasionally, so you are used to its weight and are comfortable with the way it was packed. However, if it rains while you are wearing it, you will need to unpack it completely, dry it out, and repack it.

After you have used your BOB, the same maintenance rules apply. Take everything out of it and clean away any dirt or grime that may have gotten into it during your escape. Allow your BOB to dry completely as well as any items that were in it. If you used a tent, take this out, set it up, and allow it to dry with fans blowing through it. Dry everything else as well and take an inventory. Restock items that are needed and return to your normal rotation standards for food and medications.

Keeping your BOB up-to-date

It is very important to check your BOB supplies three or four times per year, minimum. Rotating food in and out before it expires is important to ensure your escape trip is not filled with unpleasant tasting food that can make you sick. First aid items and medicines are also necessary to rotate in order to keep them fresh and potent.

As time goes on, your needs may change. Say you initially decided to use a tent because you had children and pets and were new to camping, but then your children grew, your pets died, and your experience in camping made you favor a tarp, it would be important to make sure your BOB was updated to meet your needs.

As medications change over time, it is your job to ensure your BOB contains the ones you and your family are currently taking. Update your first aid kit, not only with fresh medication, but also with accurate medication.

Returning to your home after an evacuation.
Although it may take a while, depending on the severity of the disaster, the authorities will eventually clear the area for you to return to your home. You should not try to return until you are told it is safe even if you were able to leave without trouble.

When you do return and re-enter your home, you should enter it very carefully. Only one person should enter your home to check it for safety. If you live alone, bring a friend or relative to wait outside while you are inside it, the person (or people) waiting outside need to be in a safe distance from home.

Use a flashlight that you turn on outside your home before entering. Smell for any gas leaks and mustiness. Explore all levels of your house for structural damage, animal infestations, and water damage. Check electrical boxes, wires, and gas lines for visible damage.

If everything looks and smells okay, you can turn on the lights. If anything is damaged, call a professional to examine it. It is always a good idea to clean your home thoroughly before you re-inhabit it. Bleach water mixed according to the directions on the bottle for heavy cleaning and rubber gloves are important tools to ensure your home is safe. You should not have children around while you are cleaning.

Once your home is clean, you can call you emergency contact person and inform them of your return. Unload any items, and check on your neighbors to see if any remained behind during the emergency. They may now be in need of help. And do not forget to restock your BOB. You never know when you may need it again.

Chapter 18: Obtaining the Knowledge to Survive

Survival training

Books that train you how to survive in the wilderness contain valuable knowledge to help you escape any disaster that may occur in your area. Sometimes colleges and other community centers offer basic survival courses that teach you how to identify native plants, build structures, and hunt using snares.

First aid courses are available through any Red Cross. You can also become a volunteer to help practice your skills with this agency.

Self-defense courses are available in or near most communities and will give you confidence as well as valuable skills to protect yourself. You can use these skills not only in a disaster situation, but also in everyday situations.

Practicing your skills

To practice your survival skills, you can go camping or join a group of re-inactors. You can even practice in your own backyard. Set up your tent and go camping without leaving home. Practice building a fire and then cooking on it. Or, you can use your camp stove and fix a dehydrated meal to see how much fuel it will use.

The key to practicing your skills is to do it at any time of the day and night. You should also practice in all weather. By practicing with your items, you are also testing them to see which ones work better than others. If you find a product that is excellent, be sure you include that one in your BOB.

In addition to practicing your skills, you should encourage those who may be traveling with you to practice their skills as well. Family members, close friends, and neighbors may want to prepare alongside you. If you can find a group and escape the disaster together, you will be safer. Also, groups tend to use less fuel for their fires and waste less food.

Physical preparedness

While driving away from a disaster is rather easy and requires little physical effort, hiking is a different story. Hiking involves carrying a heavy pack across the miles and keeping you moving throughout the day. It can be a very trying and demanding

Visit the doctor for regular check-ups and eat healthy foods to keep your body in shape. You must stay hydrated by drinking 6 – 8 glasses of water each day and get enough sleep at night, so you do not begin an escape fatigued. Sleep deprivation increases you chances of making careless mistakes and getting into an accident. You can prevent many minor emergency situations by keeping yourself alert. If you smoke, you should stop. Smoking takes away lung capacity and function. If you are a smoker, you will find hiking to be more difficult than it is for a non-smoker.

To begin to prepare physically, you should start taking brief walks every other day. As you go on, build up to thirty-minute walks. Be sure to get your doctor's permission before you begin any exercise programs. Even people who are disabled can benefit from exercise.

Be sure to set goals for yourself and then work toward them. You always should stretch before you exercise. As your abilities increase, add you BOB to your back and attempt to do the same exercise. When you are building your physical endurance and practicing, make sure you do not get your BOB wet. If you happen to be hiking and it starts to rain, you will need to take everything out and dry it once you are home.

You should not only train your body to increase its endurance, but you should also increase your strength and flexibility while preparing for a disaster.

Mental preparedness

Any disaster can be draining mentally. The key to surviving mentally is to know what to do. When you have gone through the motions of escaping a disaster so many times they have been ingrained into your being, you will not have to think during an emergency. Instead, you will just act. Doing takes less of a mental toll than deciding what to do because it does not require the mental anguish associated with not knowing what to do.

As soon as disaster strikes, make survival your soul goal in life. Say, "I will survive this!" and set off. When you're tired and wet and your shoulders, back, and feet hurt remind yourself – "I will survive this." Keep your eyes in front of you. Know that the journey out will not be a walk in the park. Know how to deal with difficulties that may arise on the way out, so they will not overwhelm you when they occur.

Inspirational items are another key to mental preparedness. These items keep you looking for tomorrow, so you do not have to focus on the negatives of today. When you feel like you cannot go on, take a break and spend time focusing on your inspirational items. Pray, meditate, read, or write. Do not worry about when you will get to your goal.

Finally, be sure to seek professional mental help after surviving a disaster. Professionals have been trained to help your mind release the stresses that you went through. They help relax you so that you can move past the low points and obtain higher ground.